Countertop Inspirations

EASY
CROWD PLEASERS
FOR PARTIES
120 *Tasty Recipes*

D0342132

© 2010 by Barbour Publishing, Inc.

Compiled by Marla Tipton.

ISBN 978-1-61626-012-5

Published by Barbour Publishing, Inc., P.O. Box 719, Uhrichsville, Ohio 44683, www.barbourbooks.com

Our mission is to publish and distribute inspirational products offering exceptional value and biblical encouragement to the masses.

 Member of the
Evangelical Christian
Publishers Association

Printed in China.

INSPIRATION
at your fingertips!

Looking for a simple way to bring new life to your kitchen? This book is for you. Within these pages, you'll find dozens of tasty recipes that are perfect for your next big party or get-together and are a delight to share with family and friends.

Finding a recipe is as easy as flipping through the book. At the bottom of each page, you'll see a color that corresponds to one of five categories:

Appetizers & Snacks . . . . .(p. 5)

Dips & Drinks . . . . (p. 33)

Main Dishes . . . . (p. 61)

Desserts & Cookies. . . . . (p. 89)

Breads & Soups . . . . . .(p. 117)

So set this little book on your countertop, flip page after page for fun and festive recipes, inspiration, and kitchen tips and tricks, and you might just find a little encouragement for your soul along the way. Enjoy!

APPETIZERS & SNACKS

*Praise the LORD, O my soul; all my inmost being,
praise his holy name.*
PSALM 103:1 NIV

SWEET AND SOUR PORK APPETIZERS

1 pound ground ham, cooked
1 pound ground pork
2 cups bread crumbs
1 cup milk
2 eggs, beaten
1 teaspoon salt

Sauce:
1½ cups brown sugar
¾ cup vinegar
¾ cup water
1 teaspoon dry mustard

Mix and shape into meatballs.
Sauce: Blend ingredients and pour over meatballs. Bake uncovered at 325 degrees for 40 minutes.

HOLIDAY BRUSCHETTA

2 large tomatoes, chopped
½ sweet onion, chopped
2 tablespoons olive oil
1 clove garlic, crushed
1 tablespoon fresh oregano, chopped
1 teaspoon fresh basil, chopped
2 teaspoons fresh parsley, chopped
½ loaf Italian bread, cut into 1-inch squares
¾ cup grated Parmesan cheese

••

Preheat oven to 400 degrees. In a medium bowl, combine tomatoes, onion, olive oil, garlic, oregano, basil, and parsley. Line a cookie sheet with aluminum foil. Place bread on foil and top with tomato mixture. Sprinkle with Parmesan cheese. Bake 8 to 10 minutes or until bread is browned. Allow to cool before serving.

MICROWAVE MOZZA MUSHROOMS

4 slices bacon, cooked and crumbled
12 medium fresh mushroom caps
12 cubes mozzarella cheese, crumbled
Grated Parmesan cheese

....

Place equal amounts of crumbled bacon into each cap.
Top with cheese cube. Place on microwave tray or glass
dish. Microwave on high for about a minute or until
cheese melts. Sprinkle with Parmesan cheese and serve.

COCKTAIL MEATBALLS

I pound ground beef
½ cup dry bread crumbs
⅓ cup minced onion
¼ cup milk
I egg
I tablespoon parsley, snipped
I teaspoon salt
⅛ teaspoon pepper
½ teaspoon Worcestershire sauce
¼ cup shortening
I (12 ounce) bottle chili sauce
I (10 ounce) jar grape jelly

....

In a large bowl, mix ground beef, bread crumbs, onion, milk, egg, parsley, salt, pepper, and Worcestershire sauce. Gently shape into 2-inch balls. In a large skillet, melt shortening. Add meatballs and cook until brown. Remove from skillet and drain. Heat chili sauce and jelly in skillet, stirring constantly until jelly is melted. Add meatballs and stir until thoroughly coated. Simmer uncovered for 30 minutes.

SOUR-SWEET WIENER TIDBITS

1 cup currant jelly
¾ cup prepared mustard
1 pound wieners or cocktail sausages

••

Combine jelly and mustard in top of double boiler; heat.
Add bite-size wieners and heat thoroughly.

HONEY-GLAZED CHICKEN WINGS

3 pounds chicken wings
⅓ cup soy sauce
2 tablespoons oil
2 tablespoons chili sauce (or ketchup or barbecue sauce)
¼ cup honey
1 teaspoon salt
½ teaspoon ground ginger
¼ teaspoon garlic powder (or 1 clove garlic,
    minced)
¼ teaspoon cayenne pepper

••

Separate wings at joints. Mix remaining ingredients. Pour over chicken. Cover and refrigerate, turning chicken occasionally, at least 1 hour or overnight. Heat oven to 375 degrees. Drain chicken, reserving marinade. Place chicken on rack in foil-lined broiler pan. Bake 30 minutes. Brush chicken with reserved marinade. Turn chicken and bake for another 30 minutes or until tender.

GUACAMOLE BITES

2 cans refrigerated crescent dinner rolls
½ teaspoon cumin
½ teaspoon chili powder
1 (8 ounce) package cream cheese, softened
1½ cups guacamole or 3 ripe mashed avocados
1 tomato, chopped
¼ cup bacon bits
¼ cup sliced ripe olives

Preheat oven to 375 degrees. Separate crescent rolls into long rectangles, place on ungreased cookie sheet, and press over bottom of pan. Sprinkle with cumin and chili powder. Bake for 17 minutes or until golden brown. Cool. Combine cream cheese and guacamole until smooth, spread over crust, and chill. Top with remaining ingredients.

HANDY CONVERSIONS

1 teaspoon = 5 milliliters
1 tablespoon = 15 milliliters
1 fluid ounce = 30 milliliters
1 cup = 250 milliliters
1 pint = 2 cups (or 16 fluid ounces)
1 quart = 4 cups (or 2 pints or
32 fluid ounces)
1 gallon = 16 cups (or 4 quarts)
1 peck = 8 quarts
1 bushel = 4 pecks
1 pound = 454 grams

.... **Quick Chart** ....

Fahrenheit	Celsius
250°–300°	121°–149°
300°–325°	149°–163°
325°–350°	163°–177°
375°	191°
400°– 425°	204°–218°

PITA BITES

1 bag pitas, split and cut into triangles
1 cup mayonnaise
1 onion, chopped
½ cup slivered almonds
½ pound cheddar cheese
6 slices bacon, cooked and crumbled

••

Combine everything except pitas. Spread mixture on top of pitas. Cook at 400 degrees for 8 to 10 minutes.

CHEDDAR BACON TRUFFLES

6 slices side bacon, chopped
8 ounces cheddar cheese, cubed
1/4 cup butter, cubed
2 tablespoons parsley
2 tablespoons green onions, chopped
2 tablespoons hot banana pepper rings, drained
3/4 cup toasted pecans, finely chopped

Cook bacon until crisp, drain well, reserving 1 tablespoon drippings, and set aside. Combine cheese, butter, parsley, green onions, and banana pepper rings and blend in food processor. Add bacon and drippings and process until bacon is finely chopped. Chill mixture 3 hours or until firm enough to roll into 2 dozen balls, 1 inch in diameter. If mixture softens during rolling, return to refrigerator. Roll balls in chopped pecans and store in refrigerator up to 2 days before serving. Serve with crackers.

TERIYAKI MEATBALLS

2 eggs
2 pounds ground round steak
½ cup cornflake crumbs
½ cup milk
2 tablespoons onion, grated
1 teaspoon salt
¼ teaspoon pepper

Sauce:

1 cup soy sauce
2 teaspoons ginger juice or 1 teaspoon powdered ginger
½ cup water
2 cloves garlic, minced
1 teaspoon sugar

....

Preheat oven to 300 degrees. Mix eggs, steak, crumbs, milk, onion, salt, and pepper; form into meatballs, about 1½ inches in diameter. Place in baking dish.
Sauce: Combine and pour over meatballs. Bake 45 minutes, turning meatballs every 15 minutes.

BROCCOLI SQUARES

2 (8 ounce) cans refrigerated crescent rolls
2 (8 ounce) packages cream cheese, softened
1 cup mayonnaise
1 (1 ounce) package ranch dressing mix
1 head fresh broccoli, chopped
3 roma tomatoes, chopped
1 cup cheddar cheese, shredded

Preheat oven to 375 degrees. Lightly grease a baking sheet. Arrange the crescent roll dough in 4 rectangles on the baking sheet. Bake in the preheated oven for 12 minutes or until golden brown. Remove from heat and allow to cool completely. In a medium bowl, mix the cream cheese, mayonnaise, and dry ranch dressing mix. Spread evenly over the crescent rolls. Sprinkle with broccoli and tomatoes. Top with cheddar cheese and serve.

SAUSAGE BALLS

½ pound ground pork sausage
½ pound ground spicy pork sausage
2 ounces processed cheese sauce
2 cups buttermilk biscuit mix

· ·

Preheat oven to 325 degrees. In a medium bowl,
combine sausages, cheese sauce, and biscuit mix. Mix
well and form into 1-inch balls. Place on a cookie sheet.
Bake 15 to 20 minutes.

PEPPERONI CHEESE BALL

12 ounces cream cheese, softened
¼ cup mayonnaise
⅛ teaspoon garlic powder
⅓ cup grated Parmesan cheese
½ teaspoon oregano
1 (8 ounce) package pepperoni, chopped

••

In a large bowl, combine cream cheese, mayonnalse, garlic powder, Parmesan cheese, oregano, and pepperoni; mix well. Form mixture into a ball. Chill in the refrigerator for at least 24 hours. Serve cold with crackers.

BECKY'S FAST AND EASY CHEESE BALL

16 ounces cream cheese, softened
1 jar Old English cheese spread
1 tablespoon Worcestershire sauce
Crushed nuts
Crackers or veggies

Mix cream cheese, cheese spread, and Worcestershire together until completely blended. Roll in crushed nuts and refrigerate for 2 hours. Serve with crackers, pretzels, or fresh veggies. Stores well in refrigerator.

SHRIMP DIP

⅔ cup shrimp, drained and finely chopped
1 (8 ounce) package cream cheese, softened
1 tablespoon lemon juice
Dash salt
2 tablespoons mayonnaise
2 tablespoons chili or cocktail sauce
1 tablespoon horseradish, or to taste
Dash Worcestershire sauce

....

Mix all ingredients. Serve with crackers.

LESS-MESS DEVILED EGGS

For quick and easy serving, place deviled eggs in individual paper muffin cups and set on a tray. This will avoid a mess and your guests will be delighted with a neat way to pick up and eat the appetizer.

.... Quick Tip ....

CRAB MEAT SPREAD

1 can crab meat or artificial crab meat, drained
2 (8 ounce) packages cream cheese, softened
1 cup chili sauce
Horseradish to taste

....

Mix crab meat with cream cheese. Form into a ball or
loaf. To chili sauce, add enough horseradish to give it a
kick. Pour over cream cheese and serve with crackers.

HEALTHY GRANOLA

6 cups oats (not quick)
1 cup raw sunflower seeds
1 cup wheat germ
1 cup pecan halves
½ cup coconut
1 cup raisins
½ cup dried cranberries
½ cup honey
½ cup oil (canola, corn, or vegetable)
1 teaspoon vanilla
½ cup dried apricots or other dried fruit

• •

Preheat oven to 300 degrees. In a large bowl, combine oats, sunflower seeds, wheat germ, pecans, coconut, raisins, and dried cranberries. In a microwave-safe bowl, combine honey, oil, and vanilla. Microwave 20 to 30 seconds; stir to combine. Pour over dry ingredients. Stir well. Bake 1 hour, stirring every 20 minutes. Add dried apricots during the last 20 minutes of baking. Cool. Store in airtight container. Great as cereal, over ice cream, added to yogurt, or sprinkled over fruit.

BACON CHESTNUTS

2 cans whole water chestnuts
I pound bacon, cut in halves
I cup ketchup
I cup brown sugar

Preheat oven to 350 degrees. Wrap I piece of bacon around each water chestnut and secure with a toothpick. Bake for 30 minutes. Drain fat. Combine ketchup and brown sugar to make a sauce. Pour over chestnuts and bake another 30 minutes. Bake on a cooling rack so fat can drain off.

DRIED BEEF CHEESE BALL

2 (8 ounce) packages cream cheese, softened
1/4 cup mayonnaise
1/3 cup grated Parmesan cheese
2 1/2 ounces dried beef, chopped
2 tablespoons onion, finely chopped
2 tablespoons green bell pepper, chopped
1 tablespoon horseradish
Chopped nuts

Combine all ingredients. Roll in nuts. Serve with crackers.

SLOW COOKER CHICKEN WINGS

3 pounds chicken wings
Salt and pepper to taste
1½ cups barbecue sauce
¼ cup honey
2 teaspoons mustard or spicy mustard
2 teaspoons Worcestershire sauce
2 teaspoons hot pepper sauce

Rinse wings; salt and pepper to taste. Place on broiler pan 4 to 5 inches from heat. Broil for 20 minutes (10 minutes per side). Put in slow cooker. Combine remaining ingredients and pour over wings. Cover; cook on low for 4 to 5 hours or on high for 2 to 2½ hours.

RANCH OYSTER CRACKERS

¾ cup oil
1 (1 ounce) envelope ranch dressing mix
½ teaspoon dill weed
¼ teaspoon lemon pepper
¼ teaspoon garlic powder
12 to 16 ounces plain oyster crackers

Preheat oven to 275 degrees. Whisk together first 5 ingredients. Pour over crackers, stirring to coat. Place on baking sheets and bake for 15 to 20 minutes. Makes 11 to 12 cups.

SESAME CHICKEN STRIPS

½ cup mayonnaise
1 teaspoon dry minced onion
1 teaspoon dry mustard
½ cup butter flavor crackers, crushed
¼ cup sesame seeds
1 pound boneless, skinless chicken breasts

Sauce:
½ cup mayonnaise
2 tablespoons honey
1 tablespoon prepared mustard

Preheat oven to 425 degrees. In a bowl, combine ½ cup mayonnaise, onion, and dry mustard. In another bowl, combine crackers and sesame seeds. Cut chicken lengthwise into ¼-inch strips. Dip strips into mayonnaise mixture, then into the cracker mixture. Place a single layer on a large greased baking sheet. Bake for 15 to 18 minutes or until juices run clear. Combine sauce ingredients and serve with chicken strips.

SUPER SAUSAGE WRAPS

1 (15 ounce) package prepared pie crust
48 smoked cocktail sausages

Preheat oven to 425 degrees. Unfold pie crust and flatten. Cut circle of pie crust into 24 triangles. Roll up sausage at wide end of triangle and place point down on ungreased cookie sheet. Bake for 10 to 12 minutes, until brown and done. Serve with cocktail sauce, ketchup, or mustard.

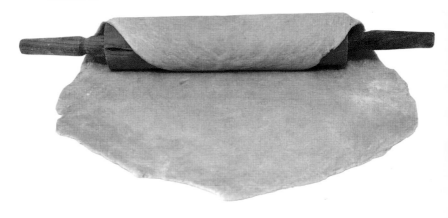

CANDLE DÉCOR

Decorating with candles is an elegant way to light up any party. Put a few on your boring countertops for visual interest, make an unused fireplace festive by placing some inside, and even put a few votives in the bathroom to keep the party atmosphere going throughout the house. Get creative in using everyday items as candleholders and let your creativity shine. Just be mindful of any children that may be at the party, and never leave lighted candles unattended.

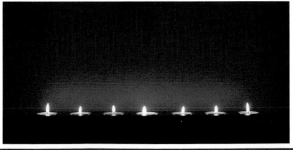

ZESTY MEATBALLS

2 pounds lean ground beef
1 small onion, grated
1 clove garlic, crushed
½ cup cornflakes, crushed
2 eggs, beaten
Salt and pepper to taste
1 (14 ounce) bottle chili sauce
Juice of 1 lemon
1 (6 ounce) jar grape jelly

. . . .

Thoroughly mix ground beef, onion, garlic, cornflakes, and eggs. Season to taste. Shape into walnut-size balls. Combine remaining ingredients in heavy skillet. Simmer 4 minutes. Place meatballs in sauce. Cook slowly 1 hour. Refrigerate till fat hardens. Skim off and discard fat. Pour into container and freeze. Reheat to serve. Makes 65 servings.

DIPS & DRINKS

Take delight in the LORD, and he will give you your heart's desires.
PSALM 37:4

PUMPERNICKEL SPINACH DIP

1 (8 ounce) container sour cream
4 ounces cream cheese, softened
2 tablespoons mayonnaise
1 (1 ounce) package dill dip mix
½ bunch spinach, rinsed and chopped
1 (8 ounce) round pumpernickel loaf

In a medium bowl, combine sour cream, cream cheese, mayonnaise, dill dip mix, and spinach; mix well. Cut out the center of the pumpernickel loaf, creating a bowl. Cut the removed bread into bite-size squares. Fill the hollowed loaf with spinach dip. Serve with pumpernickel squares.

PUMPKIN DIP

1 (8 ounce) package cream cheese, softened
2 cups powdered sugar
1 (15 ounce) can solid-pack pumpkin
1 tablespoon cinnamon
1 tablespoon pumpkin pie spice
1 teaspoon frozen orange juice concentrate

In a medium bowl, combine cream cheese and sugar; blend until smooth. Stir in pumpkin. Add cinnamon, pumpkin pie spice, and orange juice concentrate. Mix until well blended. Chill in the refrigerator 1 hour before serving. Hollow a miniature pumpkin and place dip inside just before serving. Serve with apple wedges and gingersnaps.

HOLIDAY BEAN DIP

2 (11 ounce) cans white corn, drained
2 (15 ounce) cans black beans, rinsed and drained
½ cup Italian salad dressing
1 cup ranch salad dressing
1 small onion, chopped
1 teaspoon hot pepper sauce
2 teaspoons fresh cilantro, chopped
1 teaspoon chili powder
½ teaspoon ground black pepper

In a medium bowl, thoroughly mix all ingredients. Chill in the refrigerator overnight before serving. Serve cold with tortilla chips or crackers.

CORN CHIP DIP

1 large can refried beans
1 envelope taco seasoning mix
1 (8 ounce) container sour cream
1 can black olives, chopped
2 cups cheddar cheese, shredded

....

In a small bowl, combine beans and taco seasoning.
Spread in bottom of a microwave-safe dish. Cover
with sour cream. Sprinkle olives and cheese over top.
Microwave on high until cheese is melted. Serve hot
with corn chips.

AVOCADO DIP

2 ripe avocados
½ cup mayonnaise
¾ cup cheddar cheese, grated
1 cup sour cream
2 tablespoons lemon juice

Combine all ingredients in a medium bowl. Beat with an electric hand mixer, on low speed, for 2 minutes. Cover and refrigerate before serving. Serve with tortilla chips or party crackers.

SIMPLE CRAB DIP

1 (8 ounce) package cream cheese, softened
1 onion, diced
1 can crabmeat, drained
Cocktail sauce

••

In a medium bowl, combine cream cheese, onion, and
crabmeat; mix well. Spoon mixture onto the center
of a serving tray, and spread cocktail sauce over top.
Surround dip with crackers.

CHICKEN CHEESE BALL

2 (8 ounce) packages cream cheese, softened
1 (1 ounce) package ranch dressing mix
1 (5 ounce) can chunk white chicken, drained
½ cup pecans, chopped

···

In a medium bowl, combine cream cheese, ranch dressing mix, and chicken. Form mixture into a ball. Spread chopped pecans on a piece of waxed paper. Roll the ball in the pecans until it is completely coated. Wrap in plastic and refrigerate for at least 1 hour.

KEEP A MENU JOURNAL

Consider keeping a journal of the menus you plan for your parties and get-togethers. Over the years, your journal will become a good resource so you can revisit popular menus and find inspiration for new ideas. Reserve a section to make individual lists of appetizers, salads, main courses, and desserts that you make. Add dishes in each category every time you try a new recipe. Before you know it, you will have a long list of options to choose from.

Quick
Tip

EASY PARTY PUNCH

2 envelopes fruit punch mix
2 cups sugar
2 quarts water
1 (46 ounce) can pineapple juice
1 quart ginger ale or lemon-lime soda
2 to 3 pints sherbet of choice

....

Blend fruit punch mix, sugar, and water. Add pineapple
juice. Chill. Add chilled soda. For extra-special punch,
pour over 2 to 3 pints sherbet. Makes 50 half-cup
servings.

SLUSH

1 (48 ounce) can pineapple juice
1 (12 ounce) can frozen orange juice concentrate,
    thawed and undiluted
2 (6 ounce) cans frozen lemonade concentrate, thawed
    and undiluted
Lemon-lime soda or ginger ale
Maraschino cherries

Mix first 3 ingredients together and store
in freezer in ice cream pail. When serving,
place slush in bottom of a tall glass and
fill with lemon-lime soda or ginger
ale. Garnish with maraschino
cherry.

WASSAIL PUNCH

2 quarts apple cider
2 cups orange juice
2 cups pineapple juice
½ cup lemon juice
½ cup sugar
12 cloves, whole
4 cinnamon sticks, 3 to 4 inches long

Bring all ingredients to a boil. Reduce heat. Simmer 10 to 15 minutes. Remove cloves and cinnamon sticks. Serve warm. Makes 3½ quarts.

HOLIDAY PUNCH

2 cups cranberry juice cocktail
4 cups lemonade
1 cup orange juice
Maraschino cherries
Lemon slices
3 (6 ounce) bottles ginger ale

....

Mix all ingredients (except ginger ale) together in a large bowl. Chill. Add ginger ale just before serving. Yields 18 servings.

THREE-FRUIT PUNCH

1 (6 ounce) can frozen lemonade concentrate
1 (8 ounce) can crushed pineapple
1 (10 ounce) package frozen strawberries, thawed
3 quarts cold ginger ale
Crushed ice

Blend lemonade, pineapple, and strawberries until
smooth (can be made in advance and refrigerated).
Combine with ginger ale and ice. Makes 1 gallon.

APPLE JUICE NOG

3 cups 100% apple juice
3 eggs
2 cups vanilla ice cream
¼ teaspoon cinnamon
Nutmeg

....

Combine all ingredients except nutmeg in blender.
Cover and blend until smooth; chill. Pour into glasses
and sprinkle with nutmeg.

TAHITIAN PUNCH

1 (48 ounce) can pineapple juice, chilled
1 (48 ounce) can orange-grapefruit juice, chilled
2 liters lemon-lime soda, chilled
1 pint lemon or lime sherbet

In large punch bowl, stir together juices and carbonated beverage. Spoon sherbet into bowl. Serve immediately. Garnish with citrus slices and a sprig of mint if desired.

APPLE DIP

1 (8 ounce) package cream cheese
1 cup brown sugar
1 teaspoon vanilla

Place ingredients in microwave-safe bowl. Microwave for
45 seconds. Stir. If served warm, it can be used on any
type of fruit. If served cold, then you need a harder fruit,
such as apples.

PERFECT SLICES

Use an egg slicer for an easy way to cut perfect slices of strawberries, kiwi, grapes, olives, soft cheeses, and other soft foods.

Quick Tip

BAKED BEEF DIP

2 packages dried beef
2 (8 ounce) packages cream cheese
1 cup sour cream
1 teaspoon Worcestershire sauce (or to taste)

....

Cut beef in small pieces. Mix all ingredients together.
Place in 1½-quart casserole dish. Bake at 350 degrees
for 30 minutes. Serve with assorted crackers.

BEAN DIP

3 (8 ounce) packages cream cheese
2 cans chili with beans
2 cans green chilies
12 slices American cheese

Place ingredients in order given in a 9½x11-inch dish.
Bake at 350 degrees for 30 to 40 minutes.

DESSERT DIP FOR FRESH FRUIT

1 (8 ounce) package cream cheese, softened
2 tablespoons frozen orange juice concentrate
   (do not dilute)
7 ounces marshmallow crème

•••

Combine cream cheese and orange juice concentrate.
Beat until smooth. Fold in marshmallow crème. Mix well.
Serve with fresh fruit slices.

NACHO CHEESE DIP

½ pound ground beef
½ pound ground sausage
1 onion, chopped
1 pound Velveeta cheese
1 (12 ounce) jar nacho cheese dip
1 (6 ounce) jar taco sauce
1 (12 ounce) jar salsa

Brown ground beef, sausage, and onion. In a slow cooker or saucepan, melt Velveeta with nacho cheese, taco sauce, and salsa. Add meat mixture. Serve with tortilla chips.

TACO DIP

12 ounces cream cheese, softened
1 (8 ounce) container sour cream
1 envelope taco seasoning
1 pound ground beef, browned
1 cup lettuce, shredded
1 tomato, chopped
1 onion, chopped
1 cup cheddar cheese, grated

••

Beat together cream cheese and sour cream. Spread in
an 8x8-inch dish. Add taco seasoning to ground beef
and prepare as directed. Spread beef mixture over
cream cheese mixture. Layer lettuce, tomato, onion,
and cheese on top. Serve with tortilla chips.

HOT CHOCOLATE MIX

1 (8 quart) box powdered milk
1 cup powdered sugar
1 (6 ounce) package powdered creamer
1 (32 ounce) package instant chocolate milk mix

Combine all ingredients in large container. When ready to use, put 2 to 3 heaping tablespoons in a cup and fill with hot water. Store dry mix in sealed container.

HOT CRANBERRY CIDER

1 quart apple cider or apple juice
1 quart cranberry juice cocktail
½ cup brown sugar, packed
8 whole cloves
2 cinnamon sticks

....

In a large saucepan, combine all ingredients and bring to a boil. Reduce heat; simmer uncovered for 10 minutes. Remove spices and serve warm.

FRESH BERRY PUNCH

1 (12 ounce) bag fresh cranberries, divided
3 cups water
1 envelope raspberry drink mix
1 can frozen pineapple juice concentrate, thawed
1 large banana, mashed
1 large bottle ginger ale

. . . .

Puree 2 cups cranberries. Combine pureed cranberries, remaining whole cranberries, and water in large saucepan. Cook over high heat until cranberries begin to pop; remove from heat. Stir in remaining ingredients except ginger ale. Freeze about 12 hours, stir, and refreeze. To serve: Puree slush in food processor, spoon into pitcher, mix in ginger ale.

POTLUCK PREP

Hosting a potluck dinner or picnic?
Be prepared with extra serving utensils, bowls,
and baskets for anyone who arrives without the
proper tools for serving their food. Always be
ready to act as the conductor of the food line,
and your potluck meal will be ready for feasting
in no time.

Quick Tip

GOLDEN GLOW PUNCH

3 cups unsweetened pineapple juice
3 (2 liter) bottles lemon-lime soda or ginger ale
1 quart orange juice
1 cup lemon juice
Orange slices
Maraschino cherries

....

Mix first 4 ingredients and serve garnished with sliced oranges and maraschino cherries if desired.

MAIN DISHES

"I have told you all this so that you may have peace in me. Here on earth you will have many trials and sorrows. But take heart, because I have overcome the world."
JOHN 16:33

PEPPERONI ROLLS

2 loaves frozen bread dough
8 cups mozzarella cheese, shredded
½ cup grated Parmesan cheese
2 eggs
2 packages sliced pepperoni (about 4 cups)
6 slices provolone, cut in half
Butter, melted

Thaw bread loaves individually, sealed in a gallon-size bag, at room temperature about 6 to 8 hours until dough doubles in size. Punch down and set aside. Combine mozzarella cheese, Parmesan, and eggs and blend thoroughly. Preheat oven to 350. With a rolling pin, roll out one loaf of dough on floured surface until it is the size of a small rectangular cookie sheet. Overlap the pepperoni slices in the middle from one end to the other. Sprinkle half of cheese mixture evenly over the top and then top with 3 slices of provolone. Fold each side of dough over the top and pinch edges to seal tightly. Place on greased cookie sheet. Repeat process for second loaf. Let the pepperoni rolls rest about 20 minutes before baking. Bake at 350 for 25 to 35 minutes or until crust is golden. Brush tops with butter. Place on cooling rack. Freezes very well.

CORN CASSEROLE

1 can creamed corn
1 can whole kernel corn, drained
1 box corn muffin mix
1 cup sour cream
½ cup butter, melted

Preheat oven to 350 degrees. Mix all ingredients together and pour into 9x9-inch pan. Bake 30 minutes.

POTATO CASSEROLE

2 pounds frozen hash brown potatoes
6 tablespoons butter, melted
1 pint sour cream
½ cup onion, chopped
2 cups cheddar cheese, grated
1 can cream of chicken soup
1 teaspoon salt
1 teaspoon pepper

Topping:
2 cups potato chips, crushed
½ cup butter, melted
....

Preheat oven to 350 degrees. Combine all casserole
ingredients and pour into greased 9x13-inch baking dish.
Combine topping ingredients and sprinkle evenly over
casserole. Bake 1 hour.

HAM POTATO SCALLOP

1 (5 ounce) package scalloped potatoes
2 cups boiling water
2 tablespoons butter or margarine
¾ cup milk
2 cups fully cooked ham, cubed
1 (10 ounce) package frozen cut green beans
1 cup (4 ounce) cheddar cheese, shredded

Preheat oven to 400 degrees. In an ungreased 1½-quart baking dish, combine potatoes with sauce mix, boiling water, and butter. Stir in milk, ham, and beans. Bake uncovered for 35 minutes or until the potatoes are tender, stirring occasionally. Sprinkle with cheese. Bake 5 minutes longer or until cheese is melted. Let stand 5 minutes before serving. Serves 4.

BAKED ZITI

½ (16 ounce) package dry ziti pasta
½ pound lean ground beef
½ onion, chopped
1 (28 ounce) jar spaghetti sauce
3 ounces sliced provolone cheese
3 ounces sliced mozzarella cheese
¾ cup sour cream
¼ cup grated Parmesan cheese
2 tablespoons fresh basil, chopped

Bring large pot of lightly salted water to a boil. Add pasta and cook for 8 to 10 minutes or until al dente; drain. In a large skillet, brown beef over medium heat. Add onion; sauté until tender. Drain off fat and add spaghetti sauce; simmer for about 15 minutes. Preheat oven to 350 degrees. In a lightly greased 2-quart baking dish, place about half of the pasta; top with a layer of provolone and mozzarella cheese slices. Spread on a layer of half the spaghetti sauce mixture and sour cream. Cover with remaining pasta, cheese, and sauce; sprinkle a layer of Parmesan cheese and fresh basil. Bake in preheated oven for about 30 minutes or until cheese and sauce are bubbly.

EASY OVEN STEW

1 to 2 pounds lean beef stew meat, cut into 1-inch cubes
1 bag baby carrots
1 medium onion, cut into 1-inch pieces
2 to 4 medium potatoes, cut into 1-inch pieces
1 garlic clove, minced
1 (14½ ounce) can Italian stewed tomatoes
1 (8 ounce) can tomato sauce
½ cup quick-cooking tapioca
½ teaspoon dried thyme
½ teaspoon dried oregano
½ teaspoon salt, optional

....

In a 5-quart Dutch oven, combine all ingredients. Cover and bake at 300 degrees for 2½ to 3 hours, stirring every hour, or until the meat and vegetables are tender. Serve over rice. Serves 8.

EASY ROASTED PORK

⅔ cup light brown sugar, packed
¼ cup cinnamon applesauce
1½ teaspoons ground ginger
2 pounds boneless pork loin roast

Preheat oven to 325 degrees. Lightly flour an oven bag. In a small bowl, blend brown sugar, applesauce, and ginger. Place pork roast in the prepared oven bag. Pour brown sugar mixture over roast. Seal bag and cut several small slits in the top. Cook the roast 1 hour in the preheated oven or until the internal temperature has reached 160 degrees.

GET CREATIVE!

Here's a fun way to incorporate your party's theme into your food area: Purchase inexpensive unfinished wood book shelves from a discount store and paint them with your choice of colors and theme. For example, if your party is beach themed, paint the shelves bright colors and accent them with decorations like sunglasses, a beach bag, beach ball, and flip-flops. Then serve your dishes from the shelves, making the food accessible from both sides.

Quick Tip

HAM LOAF

2 eggs
2 cups milk
1 cup bread crumbs
1 cup quick-cooking oats
2 teaspoons salt
1 teaspoon garlic salt
2 pounds ham and 2 pounds lean pork (ground
   together)

Glaze:
2 cups brown sugar
5 teaspoons dry mustard
¾ cup vinegar
....

Preheat oven to 350 degrees. Beat eggs. Add milk, bread
crumbs, oats, salt, garlic salt, and meat. Mix and form into
loaf. Mix together glaze ingredients and pour over loaf.
Bake for 2 hours. Baste often, especially last half hour of
baking time. The more you baste, the better it will be.
Keep covered until last half hour. Recipe can be made
into one large loaf, two smaller loaves, or ham balls.

EGG AND SAUSAGE CASSEROLE

6 eggs
1 teaspoon dry mustard
2 cups milk
1 teaspoon salt
2 slices bread, diced
1 pound sausage, browned and drained
8 ounces cheddar cheese, shredded

....

Mix all ingredients together, put in casserole dish, cover with foil, and refrigerate overnight. Bake at 350 degrees for 50 to 60 minutes. Serves 8.

CHINESE HAMBURGER CASSEROLE

1 pound ground beef
1 cup onion, chopped
1 cup celery, diced
½ cup uncooked rice
¼ teaspoon pepper
¼ cup soy sauce
1½ cups water
1 can cream of mushroom soup
1 can cream of chicken soup
1 can Chinese vegetables, undrained
1 can Chinese noodles (optional)

Preheat oven to 350 degrees. Brown ground beef; add remaining ingredients except noodles. Bake for 30 minutes. Stir. Place Chinese noodles on top of mixture. Return to oven and bake 30 more minutes, uncovered.

BREAKFAST CASSEROLE

4 slices bread
1 pound sausage, bacon, or ham
2 cups cheddar cheese, shredded
6 eggs
2 cups milk
1 teaspoon dry mustard
Salt and pepper to taste
Green peppers (optional)
Onions (optional)

....

Break up bread into a 9x13-inch baking dish. Layer browned meat, then cheese. Mix together eggs, milk, mustard, salt, and pepper. Add green peppers and onions if desired. Pour over casserole. Refrigerate overnight. Bake at 325 for 40 minutes.

COUNTRY BREAKFAST

9 eggs, lightly beaten
¾ cup milk
¼ cup butter or margarine, melted
1 pound sausage, browned and drained
4½ cups frozen hash browns
8 ounces cheddar cheese, shredded

••

Preheat oven to 350 degrees. With a wire whisk, mix
eggs, milk, and butter. Layer sausage on bottom of
greased 9x13-inch pan. Add hash browns on top of
mixture. Sprinkle cheese over top. Bake 1 hour.

OPEN-FACED SANDWICHES

1 pound sausage
1 pound ground beef
1 onion, chopped
2 tablespoons Worcestershire sauce
1 tablespoon oregano
Salt and pepper to taste
1 pound Velveeta cheese, cubed
Party rye bread or pumpernickel bread
....

Preheat oven to 350 degrees. Brown sausage, ground beef, and onion in skillet. Drain. Add remaining ingredients except bread. Stir until cheese is melted. Spread on rye or pumpernickel bread. Place on cookie sheets and bake until heated through, 8 to 10 minutes.

COMPANY FRENCH TOAST

½ cup butter, melted
1½ cups brown sugar
1 teaspoon cinnamon
8 to 12 slices white bread
8 to 9 eggs
¾ to 2 cups milk
Dash salt

••

Combine melted butter, brown sugar, and cinnamon.
Spread mixture in bottom of a 9x13-inch pan. Lay
bread slices over brown sugar mixture. Combine eggs,
milk, and salt and pour over bread. Cover and leave
in refrigerator overnight. Bake for 45 minutes at 350
degrees. Cool for a few minutes before cutting into
squares. Turn upside down onto large tray or platter to
serve.

VEGETABLE CASSEROLE

1 (14 ounce) can white corn
1 (16 ounce) package frozen French-style green beans
1 (10¾ ounce) can cream of celery soup
¼ cup onions, thinly sliced
¼ cup red bell pepper, chopped
½ cup carrots, shredded
½ cup grated Parmesan cheese
¼ cup colby cheese, grated
½ cup sour cream
2 cups cracker crumbs
2 to 3 tablespoons butter

••

Preheat oven to 350 degrees. Grease a 9x13-inch
casserole dish. Combine corn, green beans, soup, onions,
peppers, carrots, cheeses, and sour cream in casserole
dish. Cover top of mixture with crushed crackers. Dab
with small pats of butter. Bake for 45 minutes until
mixture is bubbly and crackers are lightly browned.
Serve immediately.

EASY SPOT REMOVAL

Two parts water and one part rubbing alcohol are the basic ingredients in any commercial spot remover—perfect for the spills left over from every party.

Quick Tip

CHINESE HAMBURGER

1½ pounds ground beef
1 stalk celery, chopped
¼ cup onion, chopped
1 can cream of mushroom soup
1 can cream of chicken soup
1½ cups water
½ cup dry rice
1 cup chow mein noodles

Preheat oven to 350 degrees. Brown ground beef and drain fat; add celery, onion, cream of mushroom soup, cream of chicken soup, and water. Mix and simmer 10 to 15 minutes; add rice and stir. Bake in a covered casserole dish for 1 hour; sprinkle chow mein noodles on top. Bake uncovered for 15 minutes.

CHICKEN CASSEROLE

1 large can green beans
1 can cream of chicken soup
5 tablespoons milk
2 or 3 cups cooked chicken, diced
½ cup cheddar cheese, shredded
Salt and pepper to taste

....

Preheat oven to 350 degrees. Arrange drained, canned green beans in a shallow casserole dish. Blend soup with milk; stir in chicken. Spoon mixture over green beans. Sprinkle with cheese; add salt and pepper to taste. Bake for 35 minutes.

EASY CHICKEN CASSEROLE

1 (8 ounce) can water chestnuts, chopped
1 can cream of mushroom soup
1 small can green peas, drained
2 (10 ounce) cans white chicken, drained
1 (8 ounce) container sour cream
1 sleeve butter-flavored crackers, crushed
½ cup butter or margarine, melted

Preheat oven to 350 degrees. Mix first 5 ingredients together. Pour into casserole dish. Sprinkle crushed crackers on top and pour melted butter over crackers. Bake for 30 minutes.

CHICKEN DIVAN

2 packages frozen broccoli spears
3 to 4 chicken breasts, boiled and sliced
1 can condensed cream of chicken soup
¼ cup mayonnaise
⅓ cup milk
½ cup cheddar cheese, shredded

Preheat oven to 350 degrees. Cook broccoli and drain. Arrange broccoli in bottom of greased 9x13-inch pan. Lay slices of chicken breast on top of broccoli. In small bowl, combine soup, mayonnaise, and milk. Pour over chicken slices. Sprinkle with cheese. Bake uncovered for 30 minutes until heated through. Can be made up the day before.

CROCK POT MACARONI AND CHEESE

1 (16 ounce) box macaroni noodles, cooked and drained
2 to 3 tablespoons cooking oil
1 (13 ounce) can evaporated milk
¼ cup butter, melted
1 onion, chopped
2 cups milk
4 cups cheddar cheese, shredded
1½ teaspoons salt
1½ teaspoons pepper

• •

Pour all ingredients into a greased slow cooker. Stir well and cook on low for 2 to 3 hours.

PIZZA-SPAGHETTI BAKE

1 pound spaghetti
1 egg
½ cup milk
1 cup mozzarella cheese, shredded
½ teaspoon salt
¾ teaspoon garlic powder
1 (48 ounce) jar spaghetti sauce
1 package sliced pepperoni
3 cups mozzarella, shredded

Cook, drain, rinse, and cool spaghetti. Beat next 5 ingredients together. Add to spaghetti and place in 11x17-inch pan. Bake at 400 degrees for 15 minutes. Remove from oven. Reduce heat to 350 degrees. Spread spaghetti sauce over noodles. Top with last 2 ingredients. Bake at 350 degrees for 30 minutes.

DEEP-DISH TACOS

2 cups dry biscuit mix
½ cup cold water
2 pounds ground beef
2 packages taco seasoning
1 green pepper, chopped
2 tomatoes, chopped
1 cup mayonnaise
2 small onions, chopped
4 cups cheddar cheese, shredded
2 cups sour cream

••

Combine biscuit mix and cold water. Spread in bottom of a greased 9x13-inch pan. Brown ground beef and drain well. Add taco seasoning, following directions on the package. Spread over biscuit layer. Add chopped pepper and tomatoes on top of ground beef mixture. Combine mayonnaise, onion, cheese, and sour cream. Spread over peppers and tomatoes. Bake at 350 degrees for 30 minutes.

SOUR CREAM NOODLE BAKE

4 cups medium egg noodles
1 pound ground beef
1 tablespoon butter
1 (8 ounce) can tomato sauce
1 teaspoon salt
1/4 teaspoon garlic salt
2 cups sour cream
1 cup green onions, thinly sliced
1 cup cheddar cheese, shredded

....

Cook noodles as directed on package; drain. Brown beef in butter; stir in tomato sauce, salt, and garlic salt. Simmer uncovered for 5 minutes. Mix together sour cream, onions, and noodles. In buttered 2-quart casserole, alternate layers of noodles and meat mixture, beginning with noodles and ending with meat. Sprinkle with cheese. Bake at 350 degrees for 20 to 25 minutes or until cheese is lightly browned.

CROUTONS IN A SNAP

Make delicious croutons for soup or salad by saving toast, cutting it into cubes, and sautéing in garlic butter.

Quick Tip

GROUND SAUSAGE CASSEROLE

1 pound ground sausage
3 cups potatoes, sliced
1 can cream of mushroom soup
¾ cup milk
½ cup onion, chopped
½ teaspoon salt
½ teaspoon pepper

....

Brown sausage; drain grease. Add it to remaining
ingredients in a 2-quart casserole dish. Bake at 350
degrees for 1½ hours.

DESSERTS
& COOKIES

How sweet your words taste to me;
they are sweeter than honey.
PSALM 119:103

SWEET PARTY MIX

1 (12 ounce) package crispy corn and rice cereal
5 ounces slivered almonds
6 ounces toasted pecans, chopped
¾ cup butter
¾ cup dark corn syrup
1½ cups light brown sugar

Preheat oven to 250 degrees. Lightly grease a large roasting pan. In a large bowl, mix cereal, almonds, and pecans. In a medium saucepan, over medium heat, melt butter and add corn syrup and brown sugar; stir. Pour the butter mixture over the cereal mixture; toss to coat evenly. Pour the mixture into prepared pan. Bake for 1 hour, stirring every 15 minutes. Allow to cool and store in an airtight container.

CHOCOLATE CRUNCH BROWNIES

1 cup butter or margarine, softened
2 cups sugar
4 eggs
6 tablespoons baking cocoa
1 cup flour
2 teaspoons vanilla
½ teaspoon salt
1 (7 ounce) jar marshmallow crème
1 cup creamy peanut butter
2 cups semisweet chocolate chips
3 cups crisp rice cereal

Preheat oven to 350 degrees. In a mixing bowl, cream butter and sugar; add eggs. Stir in cocoa, flour, vanilla, and salt. Spread into a greased 9x13-inch baking pan. Bake for 25 minutes or until brownies test done. Cool. Spread marshmallow crème over cooled brownies. In a small saucepan, melt peanut butter and chocolate chips over low heat, stirring constantly. Remove from heat; stir in cereal. Spread over marshmallow layer. Chill before cutting. Store in the refrigerator. Serves 3 dozen.

PUMPKIN BARS

4 eggs
1⅔ cups sugar
1 cup cooking oil
1 (16 ounce) can pumpkin
2 cups flour
2 teaspoons baking powder
2 teaspoons cinnamon
1 teaspoon salt
1 teaspoon baking soda

Cream Cheese Icing:

3 ounces cream cheese,
  softened
½ cup butter or
  margarine, softened
1 teaspoon vanilla
2 cups sifted powdered
  sugar

Preheat oven to 350 degrees. In a large bowl, beat together eggs, sugar, oil, and pumpkin till light and fluffy. In a separate bowl, sift together flour, baking powder, cinnamon, salt, and soda. Add to pumpkin mixture and mix thoroughly. Spread batter in ungreased 15x10x1-inch baking pan. Bake for 25 to 30 minutes.

Cream Cheese Icing: Cream together cream cheese and butter. Stir in vanilla. Add powdered sugar, a little at a time, beating well, till mixture is smooth. Frost bars with icing. Cut into bars. Makes 2 dozen.

PEANUT BUTTER BARS

1 cup butter or margarine, softened
1 cup sugar
1 cup brown sugar, firmly packed
2 eggs
⅔ cup peanut butter
1 teaspoon baking soda
1 teaspoon salt
1 teaspoon vanilla
2 cups flour
2 cups quick-cooking oats

Frosting:
¼ cup butter or margarine
¼ cup peanut butter
1 teaspoon vanilla
½ teaspoon salt
2½ cups powdered sugar
3 tablespoons milk

Preheat oven to 350 degrees. Beat together butter and sugars. Blend in remaining ingredients. Bake in greased jelly roll pan for 18 to 23 minutes or until golden.
Frosting: Cream butter; blend in peanut butter, vanilla, and salt. Add sugar with milk, beating until fluffy. Spread on bars when they are cool.

PARTY MIX

2 cups mini pretzels
2 cups chow mein noodles
2 cups crispy corn squares cereal
1 cup peanuts
1 cup raisins
3 egg whites
1 ½ cups sugar
1 teaspoon cinnamon
1 teaspoon salt
1 large package candy-coated chocolate pieces

••

Preheat oven to 225 degrees. Grease a cookie sheet; set aside. In a large bowl, combine pretzels, chow mein noodles, cereal, peanuts, and raisins. In a medium bowl, beat egg whites until foamy. Stir in sugar, cinnamon, and salt. Pour over pretzel mixture and stir until evenly coated. Spread onto prepared cookie sheet. Bake for 1 hour, turning mix with a spatula every 15 minutes. Allow to cool completely. Stir in the chocolate pieces. Store in an airtight container in a cool, dry place.

FROSTED PECAN BITES

1 pound pecan halves
2 egg whites, beaten until stiff
1 cup sugar
Pinch salt
½ cup butter

....

Preheat oven to 275 degrees. Place the pecans on a cookie sheet and toast for 10 to 15 minutes; set aside to cool. Place egg whites in a medium bowl. Fold in sugar, salt, butter, and toasted pecans. Increase oven temperature to 325 degrees. Grease the cookie sheet and spread the pecan mixture over it. Bake for 30 minutes, stirring every 10 minutes. Allow to cool completely before serving.

CARAMEL POPCORN

3 quarts popcorn, popped
3 cups mixed nuts, unsalted
1 cup brown sugar, firmly packed
½ cup light corn syrup
½ cup butter or margarine
½ teaspoon salt
½ teaspoon baking soda
½ teaspoon vanilla

....

Preheat oven to 250 degrees. In a large roasting pan, combine popcorn and nuts. Place pan in oven while preparing glaze. In a medium saucepan, combine brown sugar, corn syrup, butter, and salt. Bring to a boil over medium heat, stirring constantly. Boil 4 minutes without stirring. Remove from heat; stir in baking soda and vanilla. Pour mixture over warm popcorn and nuts, tossing to coat evenly. Bake another 60 minutes, stirring every 10 to 15 minutes. Cool and break apart. Store in an airtight container.

ENTERTAINING TIPS 101

- Allow 30 minutes ahead of time for lighting the fire, setting out candles, putting on music, and relaxing before your guests arrive.
- Always make plenty of ice ahead of any gathering.
- Always offer a pitcher of ice water at any event. It is a beverage many people prefer, and will nicely supplement any other drinks you offer.
- Clear the coat rack or entry closet of your family's outerwear and make room for guests' coats, scarves, and purses.

CINNAMON-ROASTED ALMONDS

1 egg white
1 teaspoon cold water
4 cups whole almonds
1/2 cup sugar
1/4 teaspoon salt
1/2 teaspoon cinnamon

Preheat oven to 250 degrees. Lightly grease a 10x15x1-inch pan. Lightly beat egg white; add water and beat until frothy but not stiff. Add almonds and stir until well coated. In a small bowl, combine sugar, salt, and cinnamon; sprinkle over almonds. Toss to coat, and spread evenly on the prepared pan. Bake 1 hour, stirring occasionally, until golden. Allow to cool completely. Store in an airtight container.

O'HENRY BARS

12 ounces chocolate chips
12 ounces butterscotch chips
2 cups dry Chinese chow mein noodles
2 cups unsalted peanuts

Melt chocolate in double boiler and add the rest of the ingredients. Drop on waxed paper and refrigerate.

PEANUT BUTTER FUDGE

¾ cup butter
3 cups sugar
⅔ cup evaporated milk
6 ounces semisweet chocolate chips
5 ounces peanut butter chips
1 (7 ounce) jar marshmallow crème
1 teaspoon vanilla

• •

Lightly grease a 9x13-inch pan. Mix butter, sugar, and milk in a heavy saucepan. Bring to full, rolling boil over medium heat, stirring constantly. Continue boiling for 5 minutes over medium heat, stirring constantly to prevent scorching. Remove from heat. Gradually stir in chips until melted. Add marshmallow crème and vanilla. Mix well. Pour into prepared pan. Cool at room temperature. Cut into squares.

MONSTER COOKIES

6 eggs
3 cups brown sugar
2 cups white sugar
2 tablespoons baking soda
¾ cup butter
3 cups peanut butter
9 cups oatmeal
½ pound candy-coated chocolate bits
½ pound chocolate chips

....

Preheat oven to 325 degrees. Mix all ingredients
together. Bake for 12 to 15 minutes. Let stand
1 or 2 minutes before removing from
cookie sheet.

SIMPLE CENTERPIECES

For easy centerpieces, fill clear containers or inexpensive vases with these easy-to-find items picked up at your local farmer's market, grocery store, or craft store:

- blueberries
- cranberries
- key limes
- red or yellow cherry tomatoes
- habanera peppers
- seashells
- colorful marbles

Quick Tip

FAVORITE SUGAR COOKIES

1 teaspoon baking soda
1 cup sour cream
2 eggs
2 cups sugar
1 cup butter
1 teaspoon baking powder
1 teaspoon salt
1 tablespoon vanilla
Nutmeg (optional)
6 cups flour

....

Preheat oven to 350 degrees. Mix baking soda with sour cream and add to remaining ingredients (except flour), blending well. Add enough flour for a soft dough. Roll and cut out with cookie cutters. Bake until done. Do not overbake.

COWBOY COOKIES

½ cup butter or margarine, melted
1 egg
1 teaspoon vanilla
1⅓ cups oats
½ cup brown sugar, packed
½ cup sugar
½ cup pecans, chopped
1 cup semisweet chocolate chips
1⅓ cups flour
1 teaspoon baking powder
1 teaspoon baking soda
¼ teaspoon salt

Preheat oven to 350 degrees. Grease cookie sheets. In a medium bowl, mix together butter, egg, and vanilla. Stir in remaining ingredients. You may need to use your hands to finish mixing. Shape into walnut-size balls. Place 2 inches apart on prepared cookie sheets. Bake for 11 to 13 minutes in preheated oven. Makes 3 dozen.

PEANUT BUTTER CRUNCHIES

⅔ cup sugar
⅔ cup corn syrup
⅔ cup peanut butter
1 teaspoon vanilla
4½ cups Special K cereal
1 package butterscotch chips
½ package chocolate chips

In a large saucepan, combine sugar and corn syrup over medium heat. Bring just to boiling. Remove from heat. Add peanut butter and vanilla and stir until smooth. Stir in cereal to coat and press into a greased 9x13-inch pan. Melt butterscotch and chocolate chips together in microwave or in a double boiler. Spread on top of cereal mixture. Chill until top is set. Cut into bars.

PEANUT BUTTER BARS

1 pound powdered sugar
1 ½ cups graham cracker crumbs
1 cup butter, melted
1 cup peanut butter

Topping:
⅓ cup butter
2 cups semisweet chocolate chips

· ·

Combine powdered sugar, crumbs, butter, and peanut
butter. Press into a 9x13-inch pan.
Topping: Melt together butter and chocolate chips.
Spread over mixture. Cool before cutting into squares.

CHOCOLATE COOKIES

2 cups brown sugar
1 cup shortening
1 cup milk
1 teaspoon baking soda
1 egg
5 cups flour
2 teaspoons baking powder
¾ cup baking cocoa
¼ teaspoon vanilla

Frosting:
5 tablespoons butter
3 tablespoons hot water
1 teaspoon vanilla
Powdered sugar

Preheat oven to 350 degrees. Mix cookie ingredients in order given. Drop by teaspoonfuls onto cookie sheet and bake for 10 minutes. Cool.
Frosting: Melt butter and add water, vanilla, and enough powdered sugar to thicken. Spread on cooled cookies.

POTATO CHIP COOKIES

1 cup butter or margarine
1 ½ cups flour
1 teaspoon vanilla
½ cup sugar
½ cup potato chips, crushed
Powdered sugar

Preheat oven to 375 degrees.
Mix all ingredients together.
Drop by ½ teaspoonfuls
onto ungreased cookie sheet
or form into small balls. Bake
for 15 minutes. Sprinkle or roll
cookies in powdered sugar.

PUMPKIN COOKIES

2 cups sugar
2 cups canned pumpkin
1 cup shortening
2 eggs
2 tablespoons orange juice
2 tablespoons orange peel
4 cups flour
2 teaspoons baking powder
2 teaspoons baking soda
2 teaspoons cinnamon
½ teaspoon salt
1 cup raisins
1 cup nuts

··

Preheat oven to 350 degrees. Cream together first 6
ingredients. Sift next 5 ingredients and add to sugar
mixture. Add nuts and raisins. Drop by spoonfuls onto
greased cookie sheet. Bake for 8 to 10 minutes. Frost
with your favorite cream cheese icing.

FORGOTTEN COOKIES

2 egg whites
⅔ cup sugar
1 cup chocolate chips
1 cup nuts, chopped

Preheat oven to 350 degrees. Beat egg whites until stiff
and add sugar. Fold in chocolate chips and nuts. Drop by
teaspoonfuls on foil-lined cookie sheets. Put in oven and
turn off oven. Do not open door for at least 4 hours or
overnight. Store in an airtight container.

INVITING SCENTS

The next time you peel apples, save the peels in a sealed plastic bag in your freezer. When you are expecting company, put the frozen peels in a pot of simmering water, add a cinnamon stick, a pinch of ginger, and whole cloves, and simmer gently. Your home will soon smell like fresh baked apple pie.

Quick Tip

OUTRAGEOUS CHOCOLATE CHIP COOKIES

½ cup sugar
⅓ cup brown sugar, packed
½ cup butter or margarine, softened
½ cup peanut butter
½ teaspoon vanilla
1 egg
1 cup flour
½ cup quick-cooking or old-fashioned oats
1 teaspoon baking soda
¼ teaspoon salt
6 ounces semisweet chocolate chips

Preheat oven to 350 degrees. In a medium bowl, beat sugars, butter, peanut butter, vanilla, and egg with wooden spoon until creamy and well blended. Mix in flour, oats, baking soda, and salt. Stir in chocolate chips. Drop dough by rounded tablespoonfuls about 2 inches apart onto ungreased cookie sheet. Bake 10 to 12 minutes or until light golden brown. Cool 2 minutes before removing from cookie sheet. Makes about 2 dozen cookies.

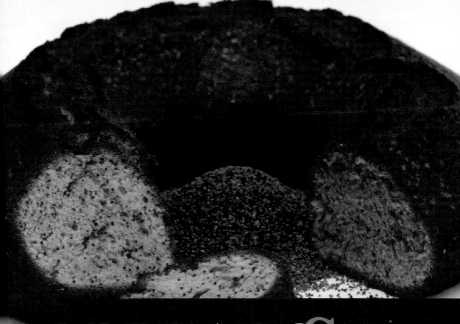

BREADS & SOUPS

Jesus replied, "I am the bread of life.
Whoever comes to me will never be hungry again."
JOHN 6:35

BLUEBERRY MUFFINS

1 ½ cups flour
½ cup sugar
1 tablespoon baking powder
½ teaspoon salt
1 egg, beaten
¼ teaspoon cinnamon
½ cup milk
¼ cup melted shortening, cooled
1 cup fresh or frozen blueberries, rinsed and drained

Preheat oven to 400 degrees. Into a mixing bowl, sift flour, sugar, baking powder, and salt. In a separate bowl, whisk together egg, cinnamon, and milk. Stir egg mixture into dry ingredients. Stir in cooled shortening until ingredients are just blended. Fold in blueberries. Spoon batter into greased muffin cups, filling each about ⅔ full. Bake for 20 minutes or until set. Freeze individually in sealed sandwich bags and then place in gallon-size freezer bags. Allow to thaw before serving.

CHOCOLATE CHIP GRANOLA MUFFINS

2 cups biscuit baking mix
1 cup of your favorite granola
2 tablespoons honey
1 egg
⅔ cup milk
1 cup mini chocolate chips

••

Preheat oven to 400 degrees. Combine all ingredients in a mixing bowl. Mix with a wooden spoon until well blended. Fill greased muffin cups ⅔ full. Bake for 15 to 20 minutes, or until a wooden pick inserted in center comes out clean. Freeze individually in sealed sandwich bags and then place in gallon-size freezer bags. Allow to thaw before serving.

PUMPKIN CHOCOLATE CHIP MUFFINS

1½ cups sugar
1½ cups light brown sugar
¾ cup plus 3 tablespoons canola oil
1 (15 ounce) can pumpkin puree
4 large eggs
3⅓ cups flour
2½ teaspoons baking soda
2 teaspoons salt
2 tablespoons cinnamon
1 teaspoon nutmeg
¼ teaspoon cloves
1 cup mini chocolate chips

....

Preheat oven to 350 degrees. In a mixing bowl, beat sugars with oil, pumpkin puree, and eggs until well blended. In a separate bowl, combine flour, soda, salt, and spices; stir into pumpkin mixture until well blended. Stir in chocolate chips. Fill greased muffin cups ¾ full. Bake for 25 minutes, or until firm. Freeze individually in sealed sandwich bags and then place in gallon-size freezer bags. Allow to thaw before serving.

BANANA CHOCOLATE CHIP MUFFINS

2 cups white flour
1 cup wheat flour
1 cup sugar
4 teaspoons baking powder
1 teaspoon cinnamon
1 teaspoon salt
1 cup chocolate chips
2 cups milk
1 cup ripe bananas, mashed
½ cup butter, melted
2 eggs

In a large bowl, mix dry ingredients. Make a well in the center. Combine wet ingredients and add to dry ingredients. Stir until just moistened. Spoon into greased muffin pans, filling about ¾ full. Bake at 400 degrees for 18 minutes or until set. Cool 5 minutes in pan. Freeze individually in sealed sandwich bags and then place in gallon-size freezer bags. Allow to thaw before serving.

CHEESE BISCUITS

2 cups biscuit mix
⅔ cup milk
½ cup cheddar cheese, shredded
Garlic powder to taste
Parsley to taste

Brush-Over Mixture:
¼ cup butter or margarine, melted
¼ teaspoon garlic powder

....

Preheat oven to 450 degrees. Combine biscuit mix, milk, cheese, garlic powder, and parsley. Mix dough until soft; beat 30 seconds. Drop by spoonfuls onto ungreased cookie sheet. Bake 8 to 10 minutes. Brush butter mixture over warm biscuits.

ANGEL FLAKE BISCUITS

5 cups flour
1 teaspoon soda
1 teaspoon salt
3 teaspoons baking powder
3 tablespoons sugar
¾ cup shortening
2 cups buttermilk
1 package yeast dissolved in ½ cup lukewarm water

Sift together dry ingredients, cut in shortening, and mix thoroughly. Add buttermilk and yeast. Work together with spoon till moist. Cover bowl and put in refrigerator until needed. Roll to ½-inch thickness and use biscuit cutter to form biscuits. Bake at 400 degrees for 12 minutes or until golden brown. Keeps 7 or 8 weeks. Makes 6 dozen.

6-WEEK MUFFINS

1 cup shortening
3 cups sugar
4 eggs, beaten
1 quart buttermilk
5 cups flour
5 teaspoons baking soda
2 teaspoons salt
1 (15 ounce) box raisin bran

Preheat oven to 375 degrees. Mix all ingredients, adding Raisin Bran last. Bake in greased muffin tins 15 to 20 minutes. Covered batter will keep in refrigerator for 6 weeks.

LEFTOVERS SEND-OFF

Invite your guests to take home leftovers
from the party by packaging food in attractive
disposable containers or doggie bags. Make
a display of see-through containers holding
fruit, veggies, dessert, or appetizers and invite
guests to select their after-party snack as they
leave. Then you won't be left with food that
might linger in your fridge.

ZUCCHINI BREAD

3 cups flour
2 cups sugar
3 eggs
1 cup oil
1 teaspoon vanilla
2 cups zucchini, grated
1 cup nuts or raisins (optional)
1 teaspoon cinnamon
1 teaspoon salt
1 teaspoon baking soda
¼ teaspoon baking powder
½ cup sour cream

....

Preheat oven to 350 degrees. Mix together all
ingredients. Pour mixture into 2 greased loaf
pans. Bake for 1 hour 20 minutes.

PUMPKIN BREAD

3 cups canned pumpkin puree
1½ cups oil
4 cups sugar
6 eggs
4¾ cups flour
1½ teaspoons baking powder
1½ teaspoons baking soda
1½ teaspoons salt
1½ teaspoons cinnamon
1½ teaspoons nutmeg
1½ teaspoons cloves

....

Preheat oven to 350 degrees. Grease and flour three
9x5-inch loaf pans. In a large bowl, mix together
pumpkin, oil, sugar, and eggs. In a separate bowl, combine
flour, baking powder, baking soda, salt, cinnamon, nutmeg,
and cloves; stir into the pumpkin mixture until well
blended. Divide batter evenly between the prepared
pans. Bake in preheated oven for 34 minutes to 1 hour.
The top of the loaf should spring back when lightly
pressed.

CHOCOLATE CHIP PUMPKIN BREAD

3 cups powdered sugar
1 (15 ounce) can pumpkin puree
1 cup oil
⅔ cup water
4 eggs
3½ cups flour
1 tablespoon cinnamon
1 tablespoon nutmeg
2 teaspoons baking soda
1½ teaspoons salt
1 cup miniature semisweet chocolate chips
½ cup walnuts, chopped (optional)

Preheat oven to 350 degrees. Grease and flour three 9x5-inch loaf pans. In a large bowl, combine sugar, pumpkin, oil, water, and eggs. Beat until smooth. Blend in flour, cinnamon, nutmeg, baking soda, and salt. Fold in chocolate chips and nuts. Fill loaf pans ½ to ¾ full. Bake for 1 hour or until a toothpick inserted in the center comes out clean. Cool on wire racks before removing from loaf pans. Makes 3 loaves.

MONKEY BREAD

1 cup sugar
2 teaspoons cinnamon
3 (12 ounce) tubes refrigerated biscuit dough
½ cup walnuts, chopped (optional)
½ cup raisins (optional)
½ cup butter or margarine
1 cup brown sugar, packed

....

Preheat oven to 350 degrees. Grease a 9-inch tube pan. Combine sugar and cinnamon in a plastic bag. Cut biscuits into quarters. Shake 6 to 8 biscuit pieces at a time in the sugar-cinnamon mixture. Arrange the pieces in the bottom of the prepared pan. Continue until all biscuits are coated and placed in the pan. If using nuts and raisins, arrange them in the biscuit pieces as you go along. In a small saucepan over medium heat, melt the butter with the brown sugar. Boil for 1 minute. Pour the mixture over the biscuits. Bake for 35 minutes. Let bread cool in pan for 10 minutes, then turn the bread out onto a plate. Do not cut; pull bread apart.

SWEET CORNBREAD

1 cup flour
1 cup yellow cornmeal
⅔ cup sugar
1 teaspoon salt
3½ teaspoons baking powder
1 egg
1 cup milk
⅓ cup oil

Preheat oven to 400 degrees. Spray or lightly grease a
9-inch cake pan. In a large bowl, combine flour, cornmeal,
sugar, salt, and baking powder. Stir in egg, milk, and oil
until well combined. Pour batter into pan. Bake for 20 to
25 minutes, or until a toothpick inserted into the center
of the loaf comes out clean.

BROCCOLI CHEESE SOUP

2 (14 ounce) cans chicken broth
1 package fine noodles
1 package frozen broccoli
¾ pound American cheese (16 slices)
4 cups milk

••

Bring broth to boil in large Dutch oven. Add noodles
and cook until tender. Steam broccoli, then add to
noodles. Add cheese and milk; be careful not to boil.
Simmer to blend flavor.

CREAM CHEESE CHICKEN SOUP

1 small onion, chopped
1 tablespoon butter or margarine
3 cups chicken broth
3 medium carrots, cut into ¼-inch slices (2 cups baby
    carrots, sliced)
3 medium potatoes, peeled and cubed
2 cups cooked chicken, cubed
2 tablespoons fresh parsley, minced
Salt and pepper to taste
¼ cup flour
1 cup milk
1 (8 ounce) package cream cheese, cubed

....

In a large saucepan, sauté the onion in butter. Add
broth, carrots, and potatoes. Bring to a boil. Reduce heat;
cover and simmer for 15 minutes or until vegetables
are tender. Add chicken, parsley, salt, and pepper; heat
through. Combine flour and milk until smooth; add to
vegetable mixture. Bring to a boil; cook and stir for 2
minutes or until thickened. Reduce heat. Add cream
cheese; cook and stir until melted. Yield: 8 servings

FRENCH ONION SOUP

4 large onions, thinly sliced
¼ cup butter
1 tablespoon flour
4 to 6 beef bouillon cubes
4 cups water
1 teaspoon Worcestershire sauce
3 slices bread, cubed and toasted
½ to ¾ pound grated cheese of choice

Sauté onions in butter until golden. Stir in flour. Add remaining ingredients except bread and cheese. Simmer 15 to 20 minutes. To serve: Place in bowl; add toasted bread cubes. Sprinkle on grated cheese, and brown under broiler.

EASY FOOD PREP

Every host and hostess wants to be able to enjoy their own party, so prepare and plan ahead as much as possible. A week before the party, prepare three or four oven dishes that will fit in the oven at the same time and that can be made ahead and frozen. Defrost your dishes prior to your party then reheat and serve. Similarly, decide which cold dishes can be made a day or two before the party. Prepare and refrigerate them.

Quick
Tip

CORN-SAUSAGE CHOWDER

1 pound bulk pork sausage
1 cup onions, chopped
4 cups potatoes, cubed and peeled
1 teaspoon salt
½ teaspoon dried marjoram, crushed
⅛ teaspoon pepper
2 cups water
1 (17 ounce) can cream-style corn
1 (17 ounce) can whole kernel corn
1 (12 ounce) can evaporated milk

In a Dutch oven or kettle, cook sausage and onion until sausage is brown and onion tender. Drain on paper towel. Return sausage and onion to Dutch oven and add potatoes, salt, marjoram, pepper, and water. Bring to boiling; reduce heat and simmer until potatoes are tender, about 15 minutes. Add cream-style corn, whole kernel corn, and evaporated milk. Heat thoroughly.

CHILI FOR A CROWD

5 pounds ground beef, browned and drained
1 (51 ounce) can tomato soup
1 (18 ounce) can tomato paste
1 (6 pound) can kidney beans
½ cup brown sugar
2 tablespoons chili powder
¼ cup dried onion
3 quarts water
Salt and pepper to taste

....

Mix all ingredients together in large stockpot and simmer several hours.

CREAM OF WILD RICE SOUP

1 large onion, chopped
1 large carrot, shredded
1 celery rib, chopped
1/4 cup butter or margarine
1/2 cup flour
8 cups chicken broth
3 cups cooked wild rice
1 cup cooked chicken breast, cubed
1/4 teaspoon salt
1/4 teaspoon pepper
1 cup fat-free evaporated milk
1/4 cup chives, snipped

In a large saucepan, sauté onion, carrot, and celery in butter until tender. Stir in flour until blended. Gradually add broth. Stir in rice, chicken, salt, and pepper. Bring to a boil over medium heat; cook and stir for 2 minutes or until thickened. Stir in evaporated milk; cook 3 to 5 minutes. Garnish with chives. Makes 10 servings.

MEXICAN BLACK BEAN SOUP

1½ pounds boneless chicken breast, diced
1 tablespoon olive oil
½ cup water
1 package low-sodium taco seasoning (dry)
1 (32 ounce) can tomato juice
1 (16 ounce) jar picante salsa
1 bag frozen corn
1 can black beans, drained and rinsed

Brown chicken breast in oil. Add water and package of taco seasoning. Simmer 15 to 30 minutes. Mix in remaining ingredients; add to slow cooker or cook on low in stockpot on stove. May serve with a dollop of sour cream and a sprinkle of shredded cheddar cheese and cilantro on top.

TUSCANY POTATO SOUP

1 pound Italian sausage
2 tablespoons olive oil
1 medium onion, chopped
1/4 teaspoon salt
1/4 teaspoon black pepper
1/4 teaspoon red pepper flakes
1 (48 ounce) can sodium-free chicken broth
1 (6 ounce) package precooked chicken strips,
    cut into pieces
1 (20 ounce) package potato cubes
1 tablespoon parsley, chopped
1 bunch fresh kale, washed, chopped into pieces

In a soup pot, crumble and brown sausage in olive oil over medium heat. Add onions and sauté for 3 to 4 minutes longer. Add salt, peppers, broth, chicken pieces, potatoes, and parsley. Bring to boil and immediately lower heat to simmer. Simmer for 10 minutes and add kale. Cover and simmer for an additional 10 minutes.

SUNSHINE SOUP

1 cup celery, chopped
3 cups potatoes, cubed
1 medium onion, chopped
3 chicken bouillon cubes
1 quart water
1 (1 pound) bag California blend vegetables
2 (10¾ ounce) cans cream of chicken soup
1 pound American cheese, cubed

In a large saucepan, simmer celery, potatoes, onion, and bouillon cubes in water for 20 minutes. Cook bag of California blend separately (don't add salt). Add to soup. Stir in 2 cans cream of chicken soup plus 1 can of water and the cheese. Heat until cheese is melted. Do not boil. Yield: 10 servings

CHEESY HAM AND RICE SOUP

⅓ cup white rice
⅓ cup wild rice
1 cup celery, chopped
1 cup onions, chopped
1 cup carrots, shredded
3 tablespoons butter
¼ cup flour
7 cups chicken broth
2 cups half-and-half
1 pound processed American cheese
⅓ teaspoon salt
⅓ teaspoon pepper
2½ cups ham, diced

In a saucepan, prepare white rice and wild rice according to package directions. In a large soup pot, sauté celery, onion, and carrots in butter; cook until tender. In a separate large saucepan, combine flour, broth, and half-and-half and cook until thick. Remove from heat and stir in cheese until melted. Add prepared rice, salt, pepper, ham, and cream mixture to sautéed vegetables. Cook and stir over low heat until thoroughly heated.

BLACK BEAN & CORN SOUP

2 (15 ounce) cans black beans, drained and rinsed
1 (14½ ounce) can Mexican stewed tomatoes, undrained
1 (14½ ounce) can diced tomatoes, undrained
1 (11 ounce) can whole kernel corn, drained
4 green onions, sliced
2 to 3 tablespoons chili powder
1 teaspoon cumin
½ teaspoon dried minced garlic

••

Combine all ingredients in slow cooker. Cover. Cook on high 5 to 6 hours.

PRE-PARTY CLEANUP

Fifteen minutes before your guests are expected to arrive, do a family clean sweep of your house, where your spouse and kids pick up all toys, clothes, shoes, and other clutter that may have accumulated throughout the house since it was cleaned for the party. Have a laundry basket handy to put all of the accumulated clutter in, and store it in a closed room or closet to sort and put away after your guests leave.

Quick Tip

BAKED BEAN SOUP

1 (1 pound, 12 ounce) can baked beans
6 slices browned bacon, chopped
2 tablespoons bacon drippings
2 tablespoons onions, finely chopped
1 (14½ ounce) can stewed tomatoes
1 tablespoon brown sugar
1 tablespoon vinegar
1 teaspoon seasoning salt

Combine all ingredients in slow cooker. Cover. Cook on low 4 to 6 hours.